Experimenting with Batteries, Bulbs and Wires

Alan Ward

Illustrated by Zena Flax

CHELSEA JUNIORS
A division of Chelsea House Publishers
New York · Philadelphia

Contents

3 5 7 9 8 6 4 2

ISBN 0-7910-1516-5

Preface

You are about to learn how to do amazing things with electricity – but not "shocking" things, because the activities in this book are safe, if they are done as described, using batteries, bulbs and wires. An electric current consists of billions of electrons flowing along a conductor, so anything electrical is also about the modern science of electronics. When you understand the ideas in this book, you will be able to extend your investigations by trying to master simple projects in electronics.

Unfortunately you cannot experiment with electric currents, unless you use batteries, bulbs and other specially made components which tend to be expensive in pocket money. But, for the projects in this book, other expenses are kept low, and various scrap materials are used. You should be able to buy the items you will need in the smaller electrical supply stores or hardware stores.

Take care only to use bulbs with batteries of appropriate voltages. Too high a voltage may cause a current that burns out a bulb suddenly. **NEVER experiment with the main electricity supply**. An electric shock from the mains can kill you. Water and electricity together are especially dangerous. People should never mess about with the main electricity supply in bathrooms or near water, unless they are fully qualified and responsible professional electricians.

The electric circuit

At the circus, performing horses go in endless circles around the circus ring. The word "circuit" is similar to the word "circus". Both words refer to a path, like a closed loop, for something to travel around.

The spinning matchbox

At a modellers' shop, buy a small electric motor that can be worked with a 1.5 volt battery cell. Fix the cover of a matchbox on the motor's spindle. Stick the motor to the edge of a table, using a blob of modelling clay.

When the two wires coming out from the motor are held against opposite ends of the battery, the motor works – and the matchbox turns. If you hold the ends of the wires against the battery *the other way round*, the matchbox turns in the opposite direction.

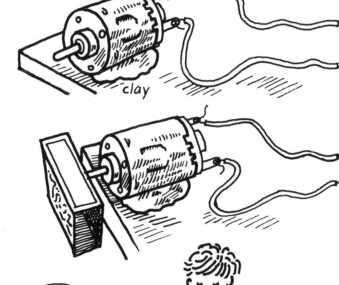

motor

clay

matchbox

motor

connecting wires with ends exposed

1·5v

1·5v battery

1·5v

Electric current can be thought of as a mysterious "something" that flows around the closed path of an electric circuit when a battery is connected as part of the circuit. The battery is the cause of the flowing. You can be sure that something is flowing in the circuit because, when the battery's connections are reversed, the matchbox rotates backwards.

An electric current is a flow of electrons

Electrons are found in the outer parts of the atoms that make up all the different materials found in the world. The central part of an atom, called the nucleus, contains protons and neutrons.

Electrons and protons are the two sorts of electric particle. You can ignore the neutrons here. A proton has a positive electric charge and an electron has a negative charge. The heavy protons tend to stay in the nucleus, while the lightweight electrons whizz around the outside of the atom.

Normally, the number of electrons in an atom is the same as the number of protons. The electrons and protons "balance" each other. Forces of attraction between their opposite kinds of electric charges help to hold the atom together. But some electrons manage to escape and wander about amongst the surrounding atoms in a material. They are called "free electrons".

In some substances, particularly in metals like copper, steel and aluminum, there are very large numbers of free electrons wandering about in all directions. The fact that they are moving means that they have energy. You can think of a battery as a pump that makes free electrons go the same way. This concentrates the electrons' energies – and so useful work is possible, such as driving an electric motor or lighting a bulb.

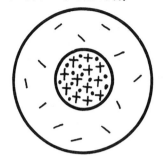

inside an atom

• **neutron**
+ **proton**
− **electron**

free electrons

Funny conductors

Hold together a spoon and a fork, a 1.5 volt battery cell and a 1.5 or 1.25 volt bulb – to make an amusing electric circuit in which the bulb lights. The spoon and fork (with many free electrons) act as a good electrical conductor.

a funny conductor (find some others)

1.5V

Conductors and insulators

Materials with many free electrons make good
conductors. Those with few free electrons make poor
conductors. The poorest conductors are used as
insulators – to make electric currents flow only where
they are wanted. Rubber, glass and plastics make
excellent insulators. They are used to cover metal
conductors, such as wires, to prevent harmful short-
circuits, and, where electric currents are very
powerful, to protect us from dangerous electric
shocks.

All the experiments in this book are done with safe
currents. That is why you can hold batteries and wires
together.

**Never try to do experiments with household
electricity. You could kill yourself.**

Inside a flashlight bulb

A flashlight bulb is a hollow glass ball containing two
wires that support a finely coiled wire filament. The
glass part is attached to a metal cylinder that has a
screw thread. Inside the cylinder, one of the filament
support wires is soldered to the metal's inside surface.
At the bottom end of the cylinder there is a black
insulating substance, through which the other filament
support wire passes, to be connected to a metal blob
on the outside.

To make the bulb light, electric current must flow in
from the side, through the filament and out by way of
the blob. (Current can also go the opposite way.)
Electrons forced to flow one way through the filament
make the atoms in the coil get so hot that they give out
light.

Break open a burnt-out bulb.
Gently squeeze it, using pliers,
just below the glass ball. You
should be able to see the things
mentioned.

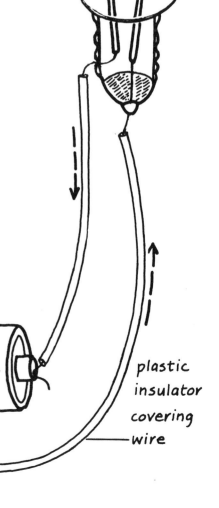

plastic
insulator
covering
wire

wire ——
conductor
exposed

6

A simple flashlight – and a tester for conductors

Get a 4.5 volt flashlight battery and a 3.5 volt bulb to go with it. (An extra volt of "push" is needed to drive electric current through the battery itself.) Tape the side of the bulb to the shorter metal terminal strip on the battery.

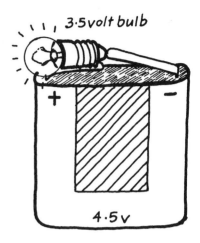

3.5 volt bulb

4.5 v

When you press the tip of the longer terminal, to touch the metal blob on the bulb, you complete an electric circuit – and the bulb lights.

By putting different materials, such as those suggested below, between the metal blob and the long terminal strip, you can test them to discover which are good conductors and which bad conductors (useful as insulators).

Test these:

paper

wood

paper-clip

chalk

pencil-lead

plastic

rubber

nail

sticky tape

coal

glass

It's done by switchcraft

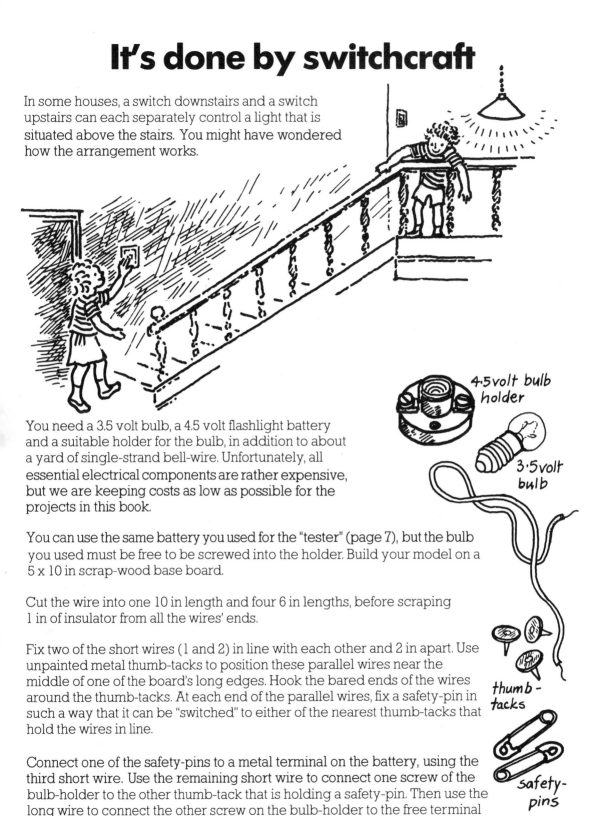

In some houses, a switch downstairs and a switch upstairs can each separately control a light that is situated above the stairs. You might have wondered how the arrangement works.

4·5 volt bulb holder

3·5 volt bulb

You need a 3.5 volt bulb, a 4.5 volt flashlight battery and a suitable holder for the bulb, in addition to about a yard of single-strand bell-wire. Unfortunately, all essential electrical components are rather expensive, but we are keeping costs as low as possible for the projects in this book.

You can use the same battery you used for the "tester" (page 7), but the bulb you used must be free to be screwed into the holder. Build your model on a 5 x 10 in scrap-wood base board.

Cut the wire into one 10 in length and four 6 in lengths, before scraping 1 in of insulator from all the wires' ends.

Fix two of the short wires (1 and 2) in line with each other and 2 in apart. Use unpainted metal thumb-tacks to position these parallel wires near the middle of one of the board's long edges. Hook the bared ends of the wires around the thumb-tacks. At each end of the parallel wires, fix a safety-pin in such a way that it can be "switched" to either of the nearest thumb-tacks that hold the wires in line.

thumb-tacks

Connect one of the safety-pins to a metal terminal on the battery, using the third short wire. Use the remaining short wire to connect one screw of the bulb-holder to the other thumb-tack that is holding a safety-pin. Then use the long wire to connect the other screw on the bulb-holder to the free terminal strip on the battery.

safety-pins

Stick the bulb-holder to the board with modelling clay, and fix the battery with rubber bands.

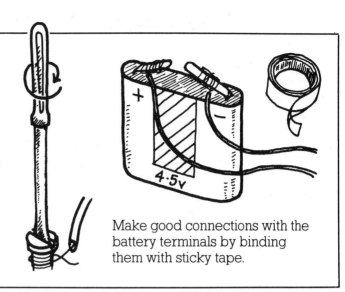

Make good connections with the
battery terminals by binding
them with sticky tape.

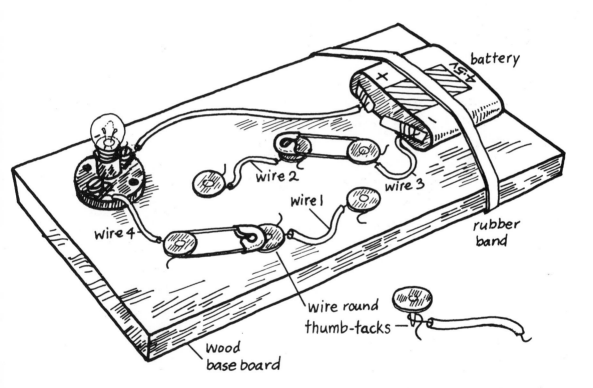

If all your connections are tight, you will find that the bulb can be turned on
and off by using either of the safety-pins as a switch.

The safety-pins represent what are called 3-way switches in America, and 2-
way switches in England. In a house, as in your model, two wires connect the
downstairs and upstairs switches. You must agree that this puzzle has a very
easy answer.

A switch and lamp set

Essentially, you need to buy a 1.5 volt battery cell, a 1.5 volt bulb and about a yard of plastic-insulated metal bell-wire. You might have to get double-stranded wire and untwist the strands.

Prepare wires measuring 16, 10 and 5 inches long. These can be cut using old scissors, but it is better to use an electrician's wire cutting and stripping tool. The plastic "spaghetti" must be scraped away from 1 in at both ends of each wire – a task made easier by the handy gadget mentioned. So the metal conductor wires will be exposed at both ends.

electrician's wire cutter and stripper

paper-clip opened out

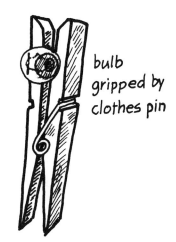
bulb gripped by clothes pin

A good size for the scrap-wood base board is 5 x 10 in. Use four thumb-tacks to fix a yogurt pot at one end of the board. Use rubber bands to fix the battery cell at the other end. Open out a metal paper-clip and fix it between the pot and the cell, using two thumb-tacks to hold it in place. The bent-out part of the clip should be poised above another thumb-tack fixed close to the cell.

Attach a clothes pin, very tightly and in an upright position, to the yogurt pot. Just beneath where the pin can be opened, fix another thumb-tack. *This tack is deliberately enlarged in the drawing.* Grip the bulb in the pin's arms, but make sure that the metal blob at the bottom of the bulb is tightly pressed against the thumb-tack behind it.

Connecting the circuit

All the wire connections must be tight. Connect the longest wire (1) between the bottom of the battery cell and the tack under the bulb. Connect the shortest wire (3) between the other end of the cell and the single tack under the paper-clip. Connect the last wire (2) between the pinned-down end of the clip and where the metal side of the bulb is being gripped by the pin.

Tight rubber bands, tacks well-pressed into the wood and contact between wire 2 and the bulb's side will ensure tight connections.

Now, when the bent part of the paper-clip (your switch) is pushed down to touch the tack beneath it, an electric circuit is completed–and the bulb lights.

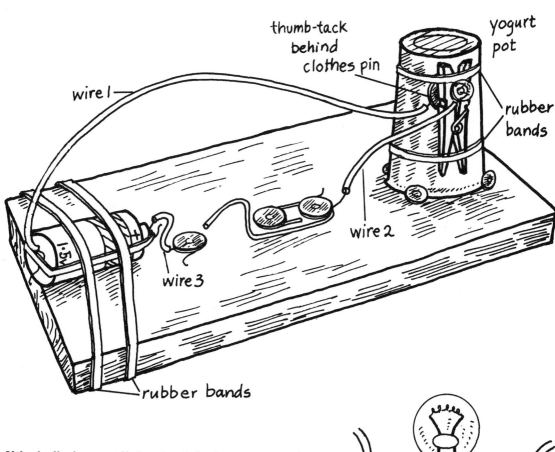

If the bulb does not light, check for loose connections (a very common fault when electrical things don't work). See if everything works when the battery cell is connected the other way round. Compare the bulb-holder that you have made with one bought from an electrician. **Why do all the switches in your house have to be insulated?**

ELECTRIC CIRCUS

Be a clown with a luminous nose

Make a false nose by cutting a quarter-size hole in a ping pong ball. Bore two little holes, one each side of the big one, into which rubber bands can be looped, to hitch over your ears and keep the false nose in place.

Use a 28 in length of thin electrical wire – perhaps taken from an old electric-bell or transformer – to connect the metal blob on the bottom of a 3.5 volt bulb with one terminal of a 4.5 volt flashlight battery. The wire can be held in place with sticky tape, but it is even better if you can get somebody to solder it for you.

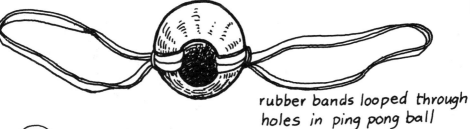

rubber bands looped through holes in ping pong ball

ie tape to attach wires o bulb

Connect the side of the bulb with a small press-switch, using a similar wire. The wire can be taped or soldered to the bulb. Then use a shorter wire to connect the switch with the free terminal of the battery.

Pressing the switch makes the bulb light. Tuck the bulb inside the false nose. Put the battery and switch inside your pocket. Operate the switch, to make the nose flash.

connect wires to press switch

connect wires to battery terminals

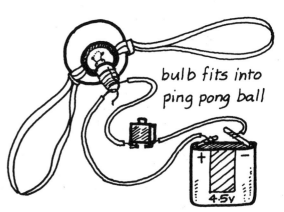

bulb fits into ping pong ball

The mystery of the winking lady

Take the portrait of a pretty lady from a magazine. Paste it on cardboard and bore a neat hole – through which a bulb can be inserted – in the center of one of the lady's eyes.

Buy a 3.5 volt flashing bulb from a motor or bicycle shop. Poke the bulb through the eye hole and screw it into a bulb-holder situated behind the portrait.

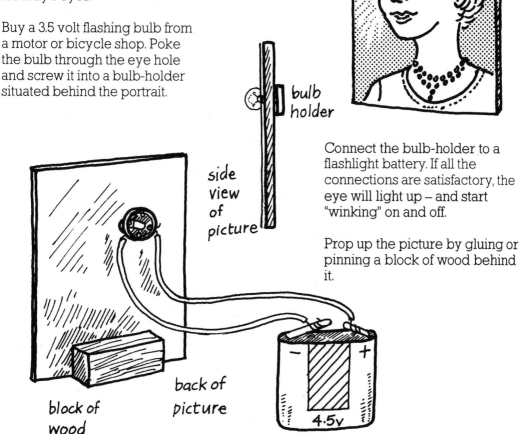

bulb holder

side view of picture

Connect the bulb-holder to a flashlight battery. If all the connections are satisfactory, the eye will light up – and start "winking" on and off.

Prop up the picture by gluing or pinning a block of wood behind it.

block of wood

back of picture

4.5v

The mystery solved

The flashing bulb contains a tiny strip of metal – which is really two strips of different metals, welded together face to face. This bi-metal strip is a clever switch. When the bulb's filament gets hot, the metals expand, but one expands more than the other one – so the strip bends and switches off the light. Then it cools, bends back, to switch the light on again – and so on . . .

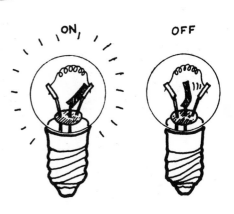

ON   OFF

Steady your nerves

Bend and twist a wire coat-hanger, to make an "obstacle wire". Push the ends into holes at opposite ends of a 6 x 12 in board. Connect one end of this stiff wire with a bulb-holder that contains a 3.5 volt bulb. Connect the bulb with a terminal of a 4.5 volt flashlight battery.

Use 18 in of bell-wire to make the final connection. Scrape 1 in of insulation from one end and 3 in from the other end, then connect this wire to the battery – but form the over-exposed part of the wire into a ring, encircling the obstacle wire.

When the ring touches the obstacle wire, a circuit is completed and the bulb lights. The object of the game is to move the ring from end to end of the obstacle wire – *without making the light come on*. Tape around the ends of the obstacle wire, to make resting places for the ring.

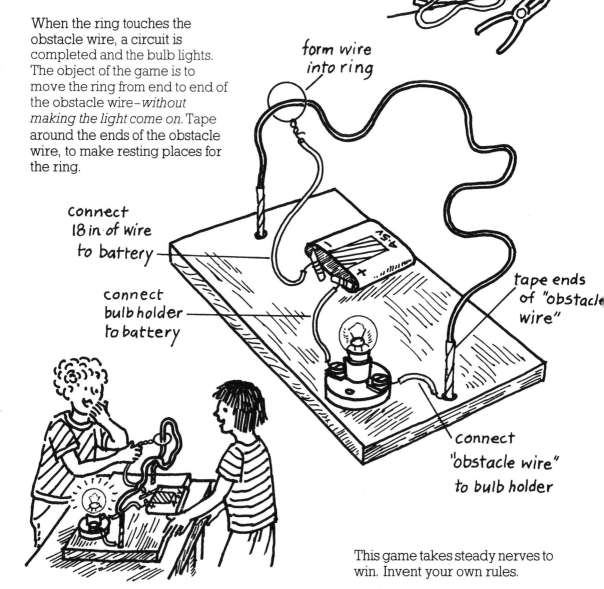

form wire into ring

connect 18 in of wire to battery

connect bulb holder to battery

tape ends of "obstacle wire"

connect "obstacle wire" to bulb holder

This game takes steady nerves to win. Invent your own rules.

Cells and batteries – how they work

A battery cell is a zinc case with a chemical paste and a carbon rod inside it. The carbon and zinc are separated from each other by an insulator. When a conductor (such as the wire shown in the diagram) is connected between the carbon and the zinc, the chemicals react with the zinc – causing the zinc to be covered with extra electrons. At the same time, electrons are taken away from the carbon by the chemicals – to leave behind many unmatched protons in the carbon atoms. So the carbon and zinc become positive (+) and negative (−) electric poles.

Electrons repel each other – they try to get away from each other, but electrons are attracted to protons. Electrons on the zinc start to push each other in amongst the atoms of the conductor. They are the force that makes all the free electrons in the conductor move one way – as an electric current. At the other end of the conductor, electrons are attracted to protons in the carbon.

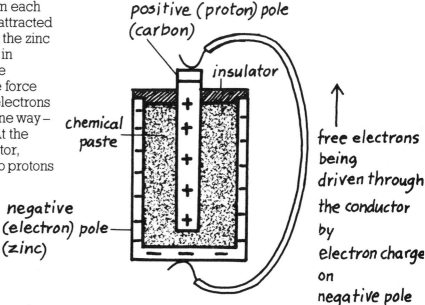

positive (proton) pole (carbon)

insulator

chemical paste

negative (electron) pole (zinc)

free electrons being driven through the conductor by electron charge on negative pole

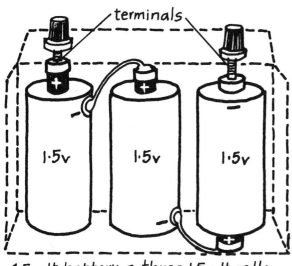

terminals

1·5v 1·5v 1·5v

4·5volt battery = three 1·5volt cells in series

One cell can deliver an electrical push of "1.5 volts". Inside a 4.5 volt flashlight battery there are three such cells. They are joined together in a series to give a combined push of 3 times 1.5 volts. You can imagine voltage as a kind of electronic pumping action.

Electric quiz games

Can you see from the illustrations how an Electric Quiz works? If the player matches the right word to the picture, the light comes on.

Notice that a 4.5 volt flashlight battery and a 3.5 volt bulb in a holder are connected, by a wire with bared ends. Two long "probe wires" lead to the quiz board. The free ends of these wires are touching spots that are actually holes in the top layer of a cardboard sandwich that has metal strips, as conductors, sealed inside. (The picture does not show the bottom layer of cardboard.)

Part of one metal strip is exposed through the hole next to the picture of a wren. The strip runs across, between the cardboard layers, to the other side of the board, and is again exposed through a hole next to the word "wren".

An electric circuit is being completed through the metal conductor strip inside the sandwich – and the light shows that picture and name are correctly matched.

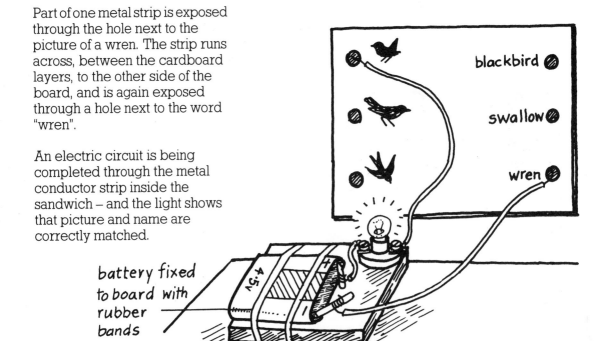

battery fixed to board with rubber bands

If the top layer of the sandwich (A) is removed and then turned over *from left to right*, it looks like B on the other side. You can see the metal strip connecting the "wren holes". Also, you can see two other strips that connect other pairs of holes. Do not fail to observe how the strips are insulated with sticky tape wherever a strip passes across the other strips inside the sandwich. If this were not done, the light would flash on for incorrect answers.

tape for insulation

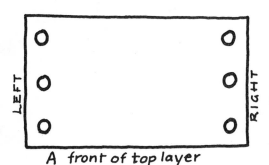

A front of top layer

B back of top layer

Use plain piece of cardboard for bottom layer.
Tape the two layers together.

Making a quiz

Fix the battery with rubber bands and stick down the bulb-holder with modelling clay, where they rest on the board.

Cut the metal strips from aluminum kitchen foil. To make everything easier to understand, only three connections are shown in the illustrations – but you will probably want to make a bigger quiz board with ten or more jumbled answers. Don't forget to use sticky tape as an insulator where the metal strips cross each other. A neat way to make holes in the top layer of cardboard is to use a paper-punch. Make up any sort of quiz you like. You could even have funny riddles to answer.

Can you make a big Electric Quiz to hang on a wall, for testing whether your friends know the positions of different countries in the world?

Bathwater alarm

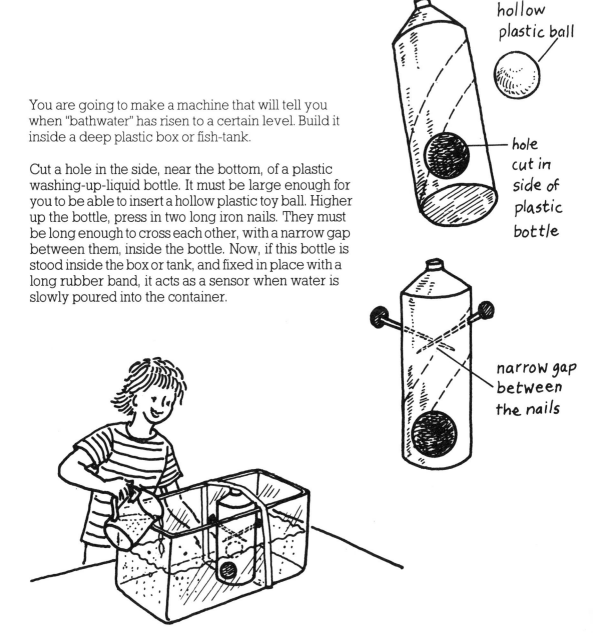

hollow plastic ball

hole cut in side of plastic bottle

narrow gap between the nails

You are going to make a machine that will tell you when "bathwater" has risen to a certain level. Build it inside a deep plastic box or fish-tank.

Cut a hole in the side, near the bottom, of a plastic washing-up-liquid bottle. It must be large enough for you to be able to insert a hollow plastic toy ball. Higher up the bottle, press in two long iron nails. They must be long enough to cross each other, with a narrow gap between them, inside the bottle. Now, if this bottle is stood inside the box or tank, and fixed in place with a long rubber band, it acts as a sensor when water is slowly poured into the container.

As the water level rises, so does the floating ball. Eventually, the rising ball pushes the nails together. Contact between the nails can make a bell ring.

Use insulated wires with bared ends. Connect one nail to one terminal of a 4.5 volt flashlight or bell battery. (The flashlight battery is cheaper, but has less capacity than the bell battery – the bell battery lasts longer.)

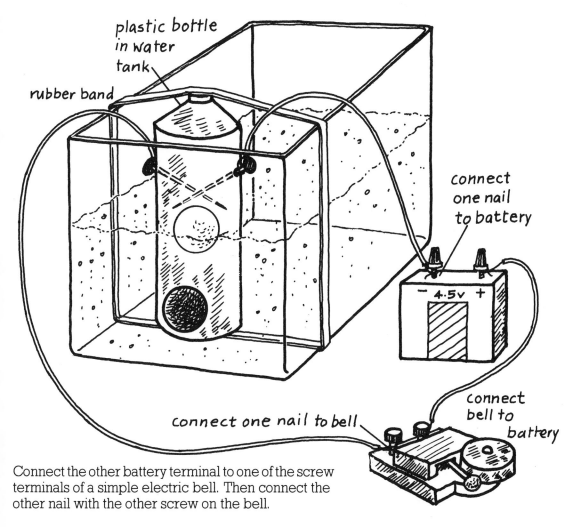

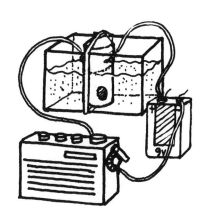

Connect the other battery terminal to one of the screw terminals of a simple electric bell. Then connect the other nail with the other screw on the bell.

Open the electric bell and see how an electrically controlled magnet coil makes the bell's striker move to and fro, to sound the metal "gong".

More fun

Invent a water-level machine that switches on a transistor radio OR invent a rain-warning machine, using an aspirin tablet sensor, that crumbles when rain wets it.

Only connect things to a battery – never to the house electrical outlets.

Fascinating circuits

Electric patience

Cut holes in the bottom of a big aluminum pie-plate. Fix the plate, upside-down, on a scrap-wood base board, using thumb-tacks. Connect one of the metal tacks with a 4.5 volt flashlight battery. Connect the other terminal of the battery with a bulb-holder (that contains a 3.5 volt bulb) and connect the other screw of the holder with a metal pair of tweezers.

Bare the ends of the wires before making connections, as always. Bind sticky tape around the tweezers, where the bare wire from the bulb-holder touches them.

If you touch the metal plate with the tweezers – *and you have good electrical connections* – the bulb lights.

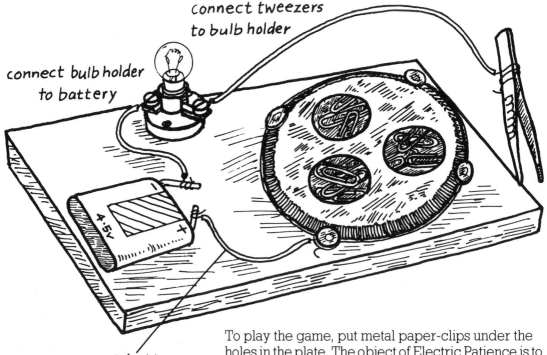

connect tweezers to bulb holder

connect bulb holder to battery

connect battery to pie plate

To play the game, put metal paper-clips under the holes in the plate. The object of Electric Patience is to use the tweezers to remove as many paper-clips as possible through the holes, in 10 seconds. Your opponent times the seconds with a watch. If you make the light flash, your opponent takes over. See who collects most clips in 5 turns – or make up your own rules.

Morse Code signalling set

Study the illustration carefully – especially where wires are connected. The bulb-holders contain 3.5 volt bulbs, and a 4.5 volt flashlight battery supplies the energy to light them.

Paper-clip switches are used on the small base boards, like the switches used for the switch and lamp set (page 10-11). Bulb-holders are fixed to the boards with clay, or small screws.

You can operate the signalling set between two separate rooms – so you will need to have long wires for **A**, **B** and **C**. Use single-strand bell-wire.

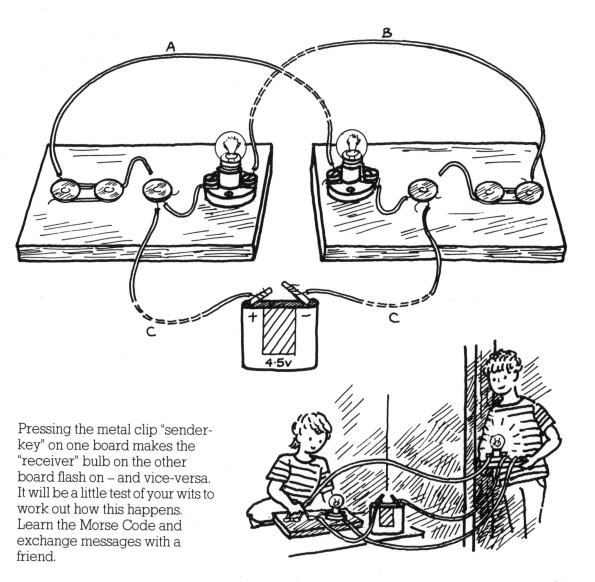

Pressing the metal clip "sender-key" on one board makes the "receiver" bulb on the other board flash on – and vice-versa. It will be a little test of your wits to work out how this happens. Learn the Morse Code and exchange messages with a friend.

Series and parallel

Bulbs in series

Christmas tree lights are connected together by wires, in series – one after another. Each bulb is part of the circuit. If one bulb breaks, or "blows", it is like turning off a switch. All the bulbs go out.

To find the dud bulb you have to keep replacing each bulb with a spare one that you know is not broken. You keep doing this until all the bulbs light up again – then you throw away the bulb that you have just replaced.

all the lights are on

all the lights have gone out; which bulb has blown?

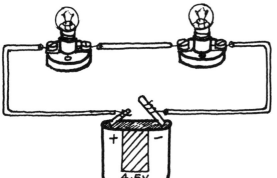

Test this idea by making a circuit containing two 3.5 volt bulbs and a 4.5 volt flashlight battery in series.

Loosening or removing either of the bulbs makes both of them go out.

It would be very dangerous to experiment with actual Christmas tree lights – so don't.

Cells and batteries in series

You know that a battery is like a pump. If you connect two 4.5 volt batteries in series, their forces are added together, making a total pressure of 9 volts. If you can afford to lose a 3.5 volt bulb in the cause of science, see what happens when you connect it, in series, with two 4.5 volt batteries . . .

what would happen?

Bulbs in parallel

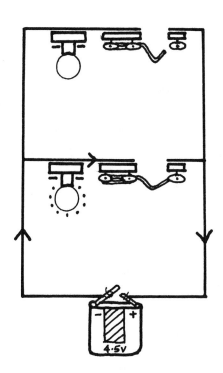

Electric lights in your home are connected in parallel. Study the model circuit shown here. Each paper-clip switch can control its own light, but not the other one. The bulbs are connected in parallel – and it should be easy to see why the word "parallel" is used.

You could build a model house with two rooms, one on top of the other, using boxes – and "wire it up" in parallel, to have a separately operated light in each room.

But never fool around with the lights attached to the electrical outlets of your home.

Cells and batteries in parallel

Cells and batteries can be connected in parallel too. If two 1.5 volt cells are connected together in parallel, they can act as one cell that has twice as much chemicals. Used this way they give a pressure of only 1.5 volts, but they can keep up the pressure for twice as long as a single cell.

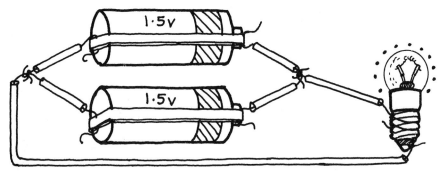

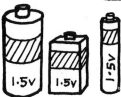

This will help you to understand why all so-called 1.5 volt dry-cells, *whatever their size*, have the same 1.5 voltage. The bigger they are, the greater their capacity – the longer they can keep pumping the electrons.

Generate electric current

Wave about a magnet, some distance above a toy compass that is resting on a table. The force field of the magnet makes the compass needle swing. This works even if you move the magnet under the table, beneath the compass.

A detector for electric currents

Cut in half a plastic-covered bell-wire that is 7 yards long. Scrape away the insulator from the ends of both of these wires. Coil one piece of wire around the top of a small jar, but leave 20 in of each end of the wire free – as leads. (You will need this small coil later.) Bind the other wire around the top of a larger jar, again leaving 20 in leads. Use sticky tape to stop the wire coils from slipping.

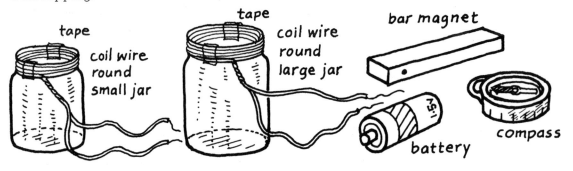

Rest the larger jar on its side. Fix the compass in the middle of the wire coiled around the jar, by wedging the compass into a big ball of clay stuck inside the jar. Turn the jar until the freely-turning compass needle stops in the same plane as the loops of the coil.

If you touch the terminals of a battery cell or flashlight battery with the bare ends of the leads, something happens to make the compass needle (20 in away) swing vigorously.

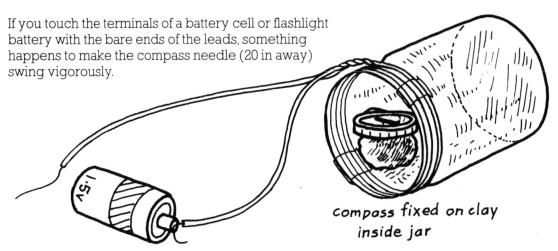

compass fixed on clay
inside jar

Does the reaction of the compass needle remind you of how it reacted to the magnet? Electricity flowing in the coil produces magnetism, *electro-magnetism* – a force field that is strong enough to affect the compass needle.

Notice what happens when you make the current flow the other way in the coil. Do this by reversing the leads' connections to the battery.

Hand-powered generators

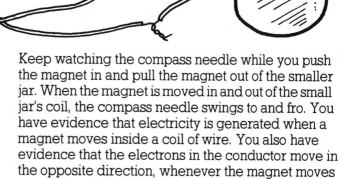

push magnet in and out of jar

Stand up the small jar. Connect its leads to the detector by twisting together the bared ends. The two jars should be nearly one yard apart.

Keep watching the compass needle while you push the magnet in and pull the magnet out of the smaller jar. When the magnet is moved in and out of the small jar's coil, the compass needle swings to and fro. You have evidence that electricity is generated when a magnet moves inside a coil of wire. You also have evidence that the electrons in the conductor move in the opposite direction, whenever the magnet moves the other way.

Your hand-powered generator produces *alternating current* – current that keeps changing its direction of flow.

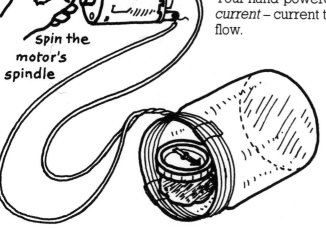

spin the motor's spindle

Connect the motor that you used for the activity on page 4 to your detector. Spin the motor's spindle. The motor used this way acts as a generator. Notice that the compass needle is deflected only one way while the motor-generator spins. This time you are making one-way-flowing *direct current*

Build an electric motor

You need thin, insulated copper-wire – from the windings of an old electric-bell or electro-magnet. Make a neat circular coil, by binding 30 turns of the wire around a broom handle. Remove the coil and flatten its windings, to make a ring shape with projecting wire ends. Keep the coil in shape by binding it *sparingly* with little pieces of sticky tape.

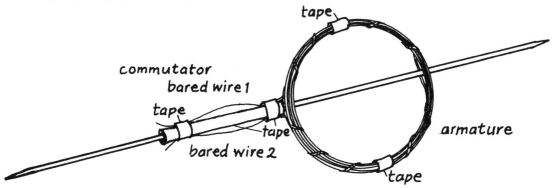

Impale the coil on a thin steel knitting needle. Insulate the bare metal of the needle near its middle, using sticky tape. Scrape away the insulation from the ends of the wires projecting from the coil. Fix the bare wire ends on opposite sides of the needle spindle, using thin bands of tape. The exposed wires are called *commutator* contacts (1 and 2) and the coil is called the *armature*.

Mount the spindle (with its armature and commutator) between two pairs of crossed nails, over a block of wood. Put a strong bar magnet just under the armature – where it will not obstruct the armature as it is spun.

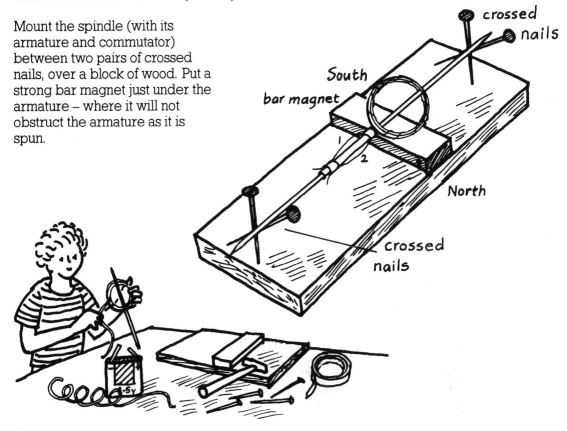

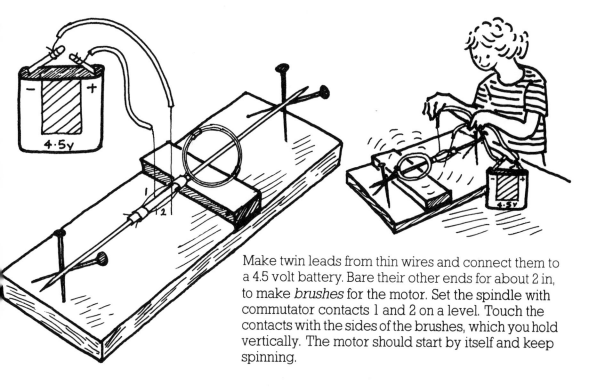

Make twin leads from thin wires and connect them to a 4.5 volt battery. Bare their other ends for about 2 in, to make *brushes* for the motor. Set the spindle with commutator contacts 1 and 2 on a level. Touch the contacts with the sides of the brushes, which you hold vertically. The motor should start by itself and keep spinning.

How it works – very simply explained

Current from the battery goes from a brush to commutator contact 1, to the armature coil and away from contact 2, via the other brush – completing a circuit with the battery. This makes the armature into an electro-magnet.

The force field of the armature magnet reacts with the field of the bar magnet under it – forcing the armature to do half a turn. Turning reverses the connections of 1 and 2 with the brushes. Reversed connections change the direction of electron flow in the armature coil – which also reverses the force field of the armature. This makes the magnets react again, forcing another half turn of the armature. These events are repeated and so the motor spins.

What can go wrong?

1 Too much friction with the crossed nail bearings.

2 A badly balanced armature coil.

3 Short-circuiting of current between wires 1 and 2 if they touch.

4 Poor battery connections.

5 The magnet placed too far away from the armature.

Can you get your motor to work with a horseshoe-type magnet?

When wires get hot

All conductors resist the flow of electrons, some more, some less. The best conductors, such as silver, copper and aluminum metals, have low resistances. Insulators have very high resistances – that is why they are used to stop electricity escaping from wires (as pipes stop water from leaking where it is not wanted).

The rate at which electrons flow in a conductor is called amperage. When the atoms in a conductor resist the pressure of voltage that drives electrons amongst them, the rate of flow of the electrons (how many per second) is slowed down – amperage is reduced – and some of their energy of motion is changed into heat energy. This is good if it happens in a part of the circuit where heat is needed, such as a bulb filament.

Another way to make a conductor hot, even a conductor that has a low resistance, is to send a "heavy" current through it – a current of high amperage.

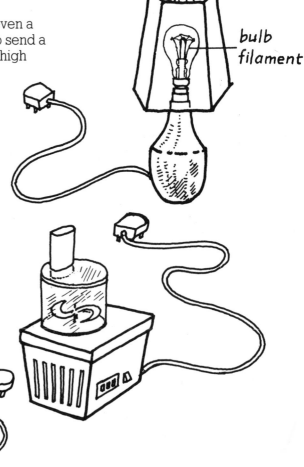

bulb filament

This can happen in the electrical system of your home, if current takes a short cut ("short-circuit") instead of going through the resistance of an appliance (space heater, light or motor) to do useful work – when the current would normally be slowed down. Short-circuits are dangerous because they can make ordinary wiring so hot that a fire starts.

Fuses are put into electric circuits to prevent wires from overheating and causing fires.

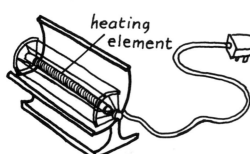

heating element

See for yourself
how a safety fuse works

A fuse is a little wire made of a metal that quickly melts and breaks at a fairly low temperature – and so cuts off the electricity supply. It is a kind of automatic safety switch.

Make the circuit shown here. Metal paper-clips are fixed to the side of the base board with thumb-tacks. Wires leading to the bulb-holder are bared at **A** and **B**. A 4.5 volt battery is used with a 3.5 volt bulb.

The fuse is a single strand of steel wool – from a soapless scouring pad. Put the fuse between the clips, before connecting the battery. Making the connection lights the bulb. Amperage in the circuit is kept safely low because electrons are being slowed down to do the work of lighting.

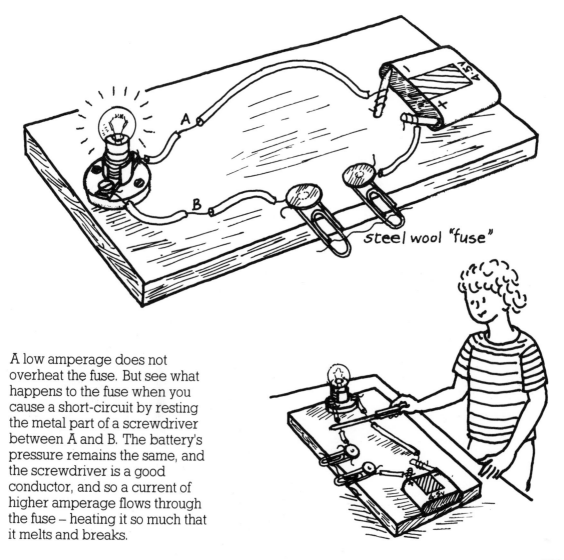

steel wool "fuse"

A low amperage does not overheat the fuse. But see what happens to the fuse when you cause a short-circuit by resting the metal part of a screwdriver between A and B. The battery's pressure remains the same, and the screwdriver is a good conductor, and so a current of higher amperage flows through the fuse – heating it so much that it melts and breaks.

The circuit breaker

Special wires called fuse wires – or capsules enclosing such wires – are incorporated in electric circuits inside buildings, to prevent electrical fires from starting. The trouble with fuses is that you have to replace them when they break, and this takes time. A more convenient device is the electro-magnetic circuit breaker. When a circuit breaker "blows", it is easily reset by a switch.

Make the circuit breaker demonstrator by putting a small electro-magnet in series with a 4.5 volt battery, a 3.5 volt bulb and a "switch" made by opening out a big metal paper-clip and resting it across the tops of a pair of thumb-tacks.

The magnet is made by winding 200 turns of thin insulated wire on a small piece of plastic tubing, cut from a ballpoint pen. (Old electric bell wire will do.) In the illustration, notice how the opened-out part of the clip rests *just* inside the tube in the coil. Sticky tape or a rubber band holds the magnet in place.

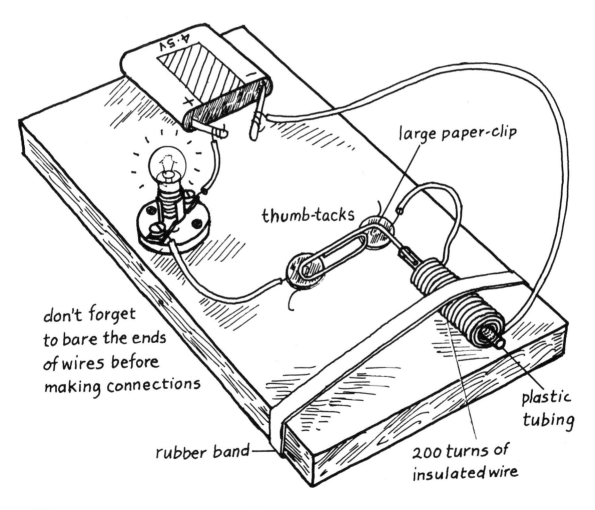

large paper-clip

thumb-tacks

don't forget
to bare the ends
of wires before
making connections

plastic
tubing

rubber band

200 turns of
insulated wire

The demonstration

Remember how the coil of the model current detector (page 24) was magnetized when current was allowed to flow around its loops. The stronger the current – that means the greater the amperage, with more electrons flowing per second – the stronger the force field of the electro-magnet.

A short-circuit reduces the resistance of a circuit by providing an easier path for the current – and therefore increasing the amperage.

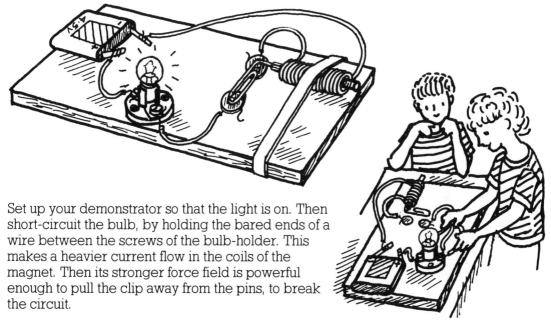

Set up your demonstrator so that the light is on. Then short-circuit the bulb, by holding the bared ends of a wire between the screws of the bulb-holder. This makes a heavier current flow in the coils of the magnet. Then its stronger force field is powerful enough to pull the clip away from the pins, to break the circuit.

Reset the model by putting the clip back where it was. Real circuit breakers work like this very simple model.

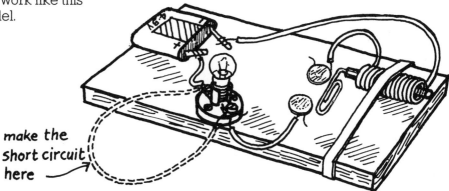

make the short circuit here

The jam-jar ammeter

Remember how the armature of the electric motor became an electro-magnet, with a force field that reacted with the force field of a bar magnet, to produce spinning. (See page 26-27.) The same idea is put to use in this model ammeter, so called because it will give you a very rough idea of how much current is flowing in a circuit.

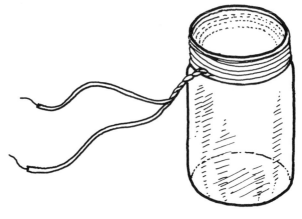

Make a tight coil of 25 turns of insulated bell-wire, by binding it around the top of a jam-jar. Keep leads, with – of course – bared ends, at each end of this coil.

Rest a cocktail stick across the top of the jar. Rest a short plastic tube, cut from a ballpoint pen, between the rim of the jar and the stick – and put a tight rubber band around the jar, to hold the tube in place.

plastic tube
rubber band
stick

bend straw down

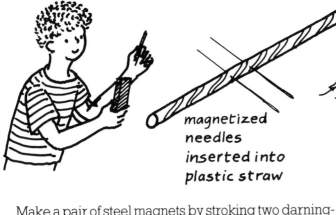

magnetized needles inserted into plastic straw

Make a pair of steel magnets by stroking two darning-needles, from heads to points only, using one end of a powerful bar magnet. The steel needles, unlike your various electro-magnets, will retain their magnetism. Insert these needles, to balance, side by side, near the middle of a plastic straw. They must be at 90° with the straw – and they must be horizontal when an end of the straw is bent down, to make a pointer. Mount the other end of the straw inside the plastic tube. The pointer should now dangle down and the needle magnets should be horizontal.

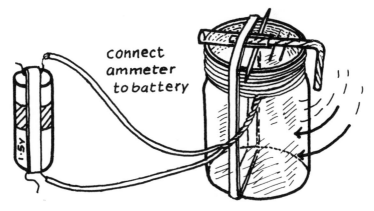

connect ammeter to battery

If you connect the leads from your ammeter to a battery, the coil becomes an electro-magnet. This temporary magnet interacts with the permanent steel needle magnets, making the needles turn – and making the pointer turn too. The stronger the current, the stronger the magnetism of the coil – and the greater the degree of swing of the pointer.

Tests with the ammeter

1 See what happens when you connect the leads to the battery the other way round.

2 See what happens when you connect one 1.5 volt cell to the ammeter. Then see what happens when you connect two cells, in series.

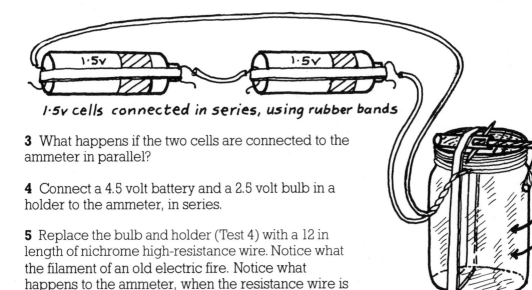

1·5v cells connected in series, using rubber bands

3 What happens if the two cells are connected to the ammeter in parallel?

4 Connect a 4.5 volt battery and a 2.5 volt bulb in a holder to the ammeter, in series.

5 Replace the bulb and holder (Test 4) with a 12 in length of nichrome high-resistance wire. Notice what the filament of an old electric fire. Notice what happens to the ammeter, when the resistance wire is scraped across one of the battery terminals, while it is in a series circuit with the ammeter.

Try to explain your observations. **Never be tempted to try connecting your apparatus to the electrical outlets of your house.**

Buzzer to bell

Wind 100 turns of thin insulated wire on to a 2 in long iron bolt which has a nut opposite its head end. Use small nails to form a rough "cage" to grip the bolt firmly near the edge of a base board.

Use old scissors to cut a 0.5 x 3 in strip of tinned iron from a food can. **Take great care not to cut yourself**. Use pliers to help you bend ¾ in of this strip tightly around a nail that is about 1 inch long. Impale a thin iron nut on this nail, before hammering the nail into the board – doing this in such a way that the springy end of the metal is just in front of the wire-wound bolt.

Connect one of the bared ends of the wire from the windings to the nail holding the springy metal. Connect the other end to one of a pair of tacked-down paper-clips.

Connect the other of this pair of paper-clips to another tacked-down clip, which has one of its ends opened out. The opened end of this clip will make contact with the metal strip, opposite to where the strip almost touches the head of the rigidly held bolt.

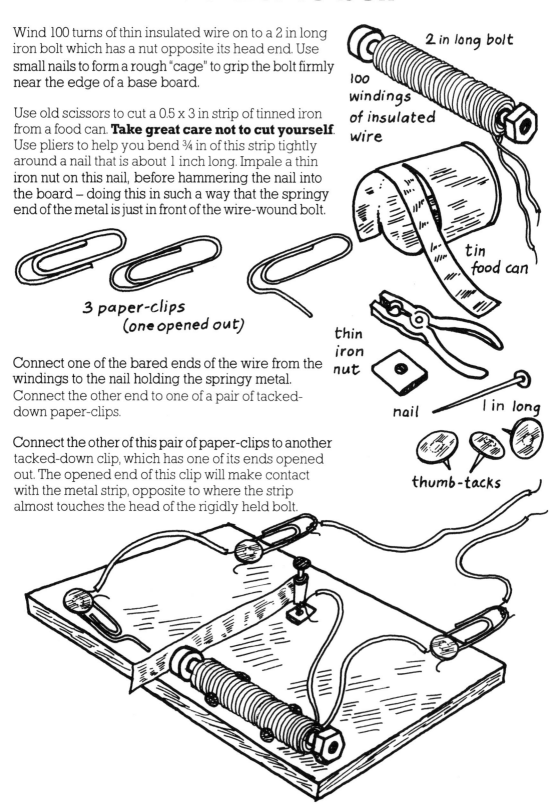

2 in long bolt

100 windings of insulated wire

tin food can

3 paper-clips (one opened out)

thin iron nut

nail

1 in long

thumb-tacks

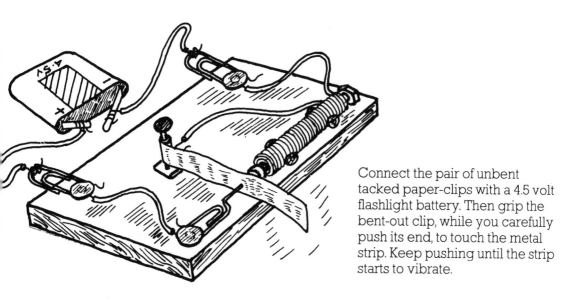

Connect the pair of unbent tacked paper-clips with a 4.5 volt flashlight battery. Then grip the bent-out clip, while you carefully push its end, to touch the metal strip. Keep pushing until the strip starts to vibrate.

The make-and-break cycle of action

Making the connection with the metal strip completes an electric circuit through the insulated coil of windings on the iron bolt. This makes the bolt act as an electro-magnet. The magnet attracts the strip, but this action breaks the connection with the clip – and switches off the current. So the electro-magnet loses its power. The metal strip, released from the magnet, flips back to make contact with the clip again – and the cycle is repeated, with the vibrating strip buzzing away . . .

If you look inside a disconnected electric bell, you should be able to work out how the make-and-break principle makes the bell ring.

Ringing tones

Convert your buzzer into a model bell. Put a small clipboard-clip on the end of the springy strip. Stand a glass tumbler, upside-down, on top of a toy brick – just in front of the clipboard-clip "striker". The tumbler must not touch the table. Operate the make-and-break mechanism – and listen to the ringing tones of your glass bell.

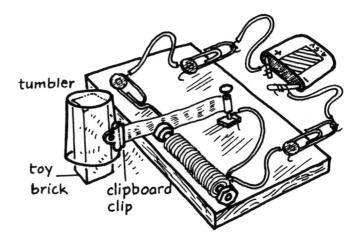

tumbler

toy brick

clipboard clip

Electro-magnetic lab: Part 1

The needle of a compass is a magnet. Allowed to swing and settle on its pivot, in a place where there are no iron or other magnetic objects to influence it, the magnetic compass needle points along a North-South line. The end of the magnet that points to North (actually to Magnetic North which is not quite the same direction as true Geographical North) is called its North-seeking pole. Its opposite pole is a South-seeking pole. These poles are usually described simply as north and south poles.

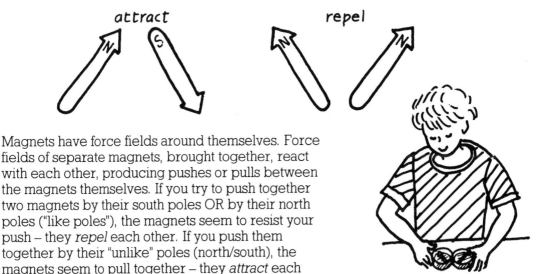

attract   *repel*

Magnets have force fields around themselves. Force fields of separate magnets, brought together, react with each other, producing pushes or pulls between the magnets themselves. If you try to push together two magnets by their south poles OR by their north poles ("like poles"), the magnets seem to resist your push – they *repel* each other. If you push them together by their "unlike" poles (north/south), the magnets seem to pull together – they *attract* each other. These effects are called the Laws of Magnetism.

Electricity produces magnetism

Fix a 4.5 volt flashlight battery, in series, with a paper-clip switch and two thumb-tacks, using a wooden base board. Bare the ends of a yard of plastic-covered bell-wire. Thread this wire through the plastic tube from an old ballpoint pen. Tape the exposed ends of this wire to the tops of the metal tacks.

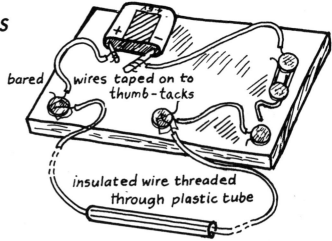

bared / wires taped on to thumb-tacks

insulated wire threaded through plastic tube

By pressing the switch, you can send bursts of current through the wire. Do not keep the wire electrified for long, because it has a low resistance, and keeping it connected soon uses up the energy from the battery. (The chemicals in the battery will finish their reactions too quickly.)

Testing

Fix a wooden tile over a large wooden block, using modelling clay to hold it, to form a ledge. Both these wooden pieces can be toy bricks. Put a toy compass on the ledge.

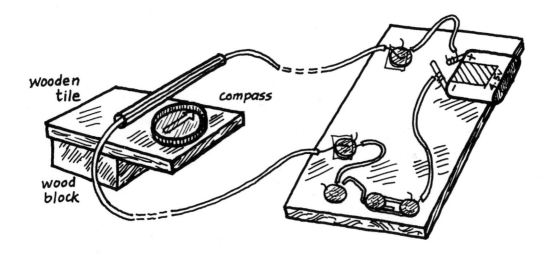

You already know that electricity produces magnetism. Now you can study the effects of this magnetism in more detail. The plastic tube makes it easy for you to hold a section of the wire above or below the compass. Line up the compass needle with the wire for all your experiments.

What happens to the compass when:

1 The electrified wire is held just above it?

2 The wire is held just underneath it?

3 The wire is held further away from the compass (above, sideways and below)?

4 1, 2 and 3 are repeated with the direction of the current reversed?

These observations will give you some ideas about the invisible forces at work, when two magnetic fields interact.

Electro-magnetic lab: Part 2

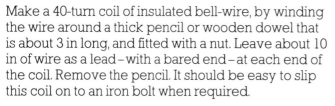

Make a 40-turn coil of insulated bell-wire, by winding the wire around a thick pencil or wooden dowel that is about 3 in long, and fitted with a nut. Leave about 10 in of wire as a lead – with a bared end – at each end of the coil. Remove the pencil. It should be easy to slip this coil on to an iron bolt when required.

Connect the 40-turn coil with the thumb-tacks on the base board (used in Part 1). Put the coil near the compass. Electrify the coil with short bursts of current. You will control the current by pressing the clip switch for half a second at a time.

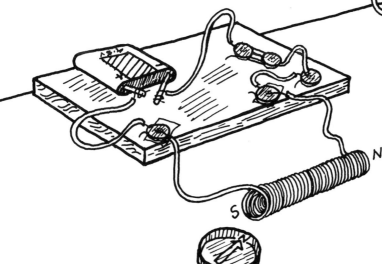

Notice what happens to the compass needle. The coil acts as a weak magnet. Its force field interacts with the permanent magnet's field – to make the needle swing.

Electro-magnets with only coils – with nothing inside the coils – are called solenoids.

Use the north pole of the compass as a reference, to help you to identify the north and south poles of the solenoid magnet – while the current is flowing. Apply the Laws of Magnetism.

What might you expect to happen to the poles of the solenoid magnet, if the current is reversed? Try this – and check your prediction.

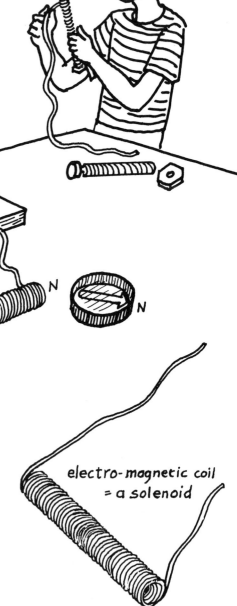

electro-magnetic coil = a solenoid

Impale the 40-turn coil upon a thin iron bolt, fixing it there by screwing on the nut. The bolt gives the coil an iron core. Connect the coil with the thumb-tacks on the base board. Put the electro-magnet near the compass. Tap the switch. When current flows you will notice that adding the iron core makes the electro-magnet more powerful.

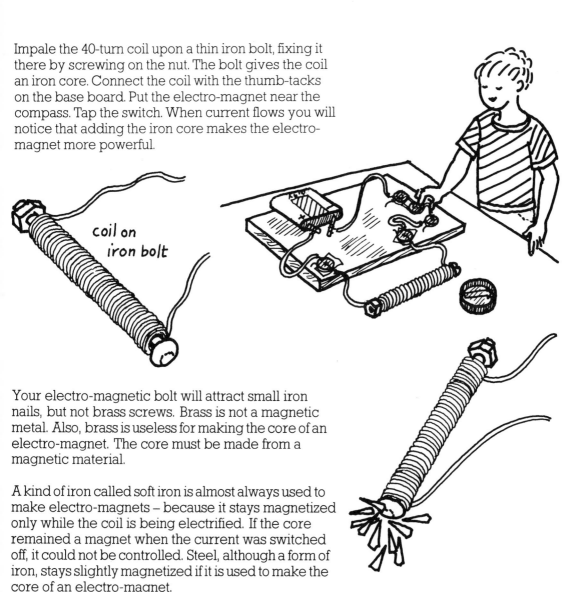

coil on
iron bolt

Your electro-magnetic bolt will attract small iron nails, but not brass screws. Brass is not a magnetic metal. Also, brass is useless for making the core of an electro-magnet. The core must be made from a magnetic material.

A kind of iron called soft iron is almost always used to make electro-magnets – because it stays magnetized only while the coil is being electrified. If the core remained a magnet when the current was switched off, it could not be controlled. Steel, although a form of iron, stays slightly magnetized if it is used to make the core of an electro-magnet.

Research project

Plan and do tests to find out how varying the strength of an electric current affects the strength of an electro-magnet. You could do this by first using a 1.5 volt battery cell, and then using it in series with another 1.5 volt cell, to double the voltage driving the current.

Also, compare the numbers of small iron nails attracted by an electro-magnet when the number of turns used in the coil is increased or made less.

A solenoid-controlled signal

Build a model signal, to show the principle of "tube" electro-magnets, or solenoids. These are often used in electrical and electronic machinery. Solenoids were used to work turn signals in older motor-cars.

Use a wooden ruler for the signal's supporting post. Make the signalling arm by pinning a 10 x 0.5 x 0.5 inch balsa-wood strip (from a modellers' shop) on one end of the ruler. Impale a small bead on the tack "pivot", before fixing the signal arm to the ruler.

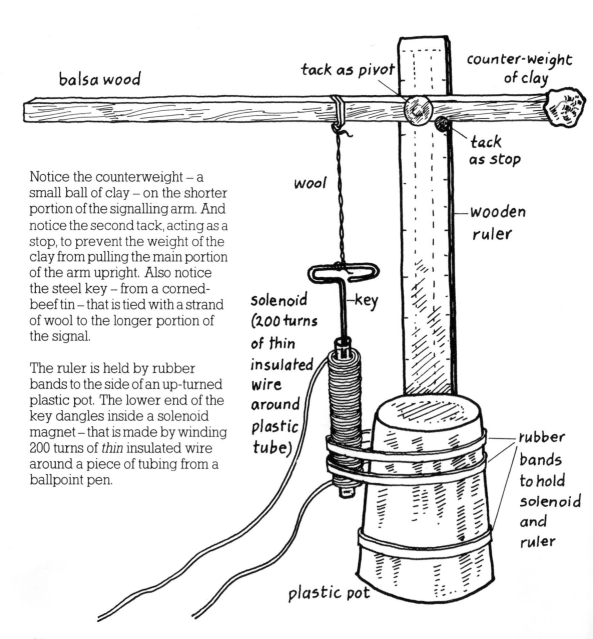

balsa wood

tack as pivot

counter-weight of clay

wool

tack as stop

wooden ruler

solenoid (200 turns of thin insulated wire around plastic tube)

key

rubber bands to hold solenoid and ruler

plastic pot

Notice the counterweight – a small ball of clay – on the shorter portion of the signalling arm. And notice the second tack, acting as a stop, to prevent the weight of the clay from pulling the main portion of the arm upright. Also notice the steel key – from a corned-beef tin – that is tied with a strand of wool to the longer portion of the signal.

The ruler is held by rubber bands to the side of an up-turned plastic pot. The lower end of the key dangles inside a solenoid magnet – that is made by winding 200 turns of *thin* insulated wire around a piece of tubing from a ballpoint pen.

The solenoid is connected in series with a 4.5 volt flashlight battery and a switch. Make the spring-switch from a clothes pin. Steel paper-clips, with bent ends, are taped to the prongs of the pin.

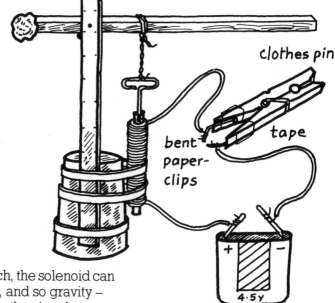

By squeezing the prongs you make the bent parts of the clips touch, to complete an electric circuit. Then the solenoid is activated, to pull the metal key inside – and force the signal to dip down.

When you stop squeezing the switch, the solenoid can no longer exert a force on the key, and so gravity – acting on the counterweight – pulls the signal up.

Something to think about

The magnetic field of the solenoid magnetizes the steel key. The key, becoming magnetized, acquires a force field of its own. The two force fields overlap and act as one. The unified field tends to contract, or shorten – so the part of the field surrounding the mobile key is pulled towards the solenoid. This is the force that works the signal.

The force field around a solenoid seems to be made of lines, along which an imaginary "magnetic flux" flows, as the arrows suggest.

Electro-magnetic games

Dancing Alek Tron

Make an electro-magnet by winding at least 50 turns of insulated bell-wire around a 2 in iron bolt. Bore a hole in a base board, into which the end of the bolt can be firmly wedged.

Find a small cardboard box to just cover the head of the bolt. The box will be upside-down. Fix a strong wire gallows shape into the board and hang from it a cut-out cardboard puppet, to which are attached two pairs of linked paper-clips, as metal legs. The legs should dangle just above the concealed magnet.

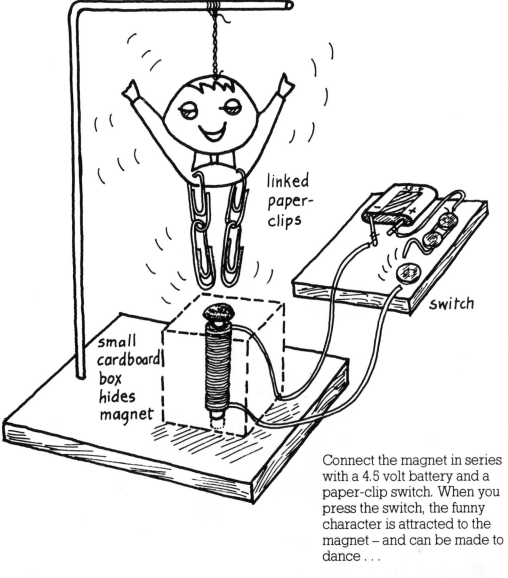

linked paper-clips

switch

small cardboard box hides magnet

Connect the magnet in series with a 4.5 volt battery and a paper-clip switch. When you press the switch, the funny character is attracted to the magnet – and can be made to dance . . .

Magnetic catapult

Wind a solenoid of about 100 turns of thin insulated wire, on a 2 in long plastic tube. Connect one lead from the solenoid to a terminal of a 4.5 volt battery. Tape the magnet to a base board.

Insert a steel pin about a third of its length inside the solenoid. Then just brush the other lead from the magnet against the other terminal of the battery.

During the instant that the coil is a magnet, the pin is pulled into the tube and accelerated. With practice, you can make the pin shoot for a distance of several inches beyond the other end of the tube.

Invent a shooting game, based upon the magnetic catapult.

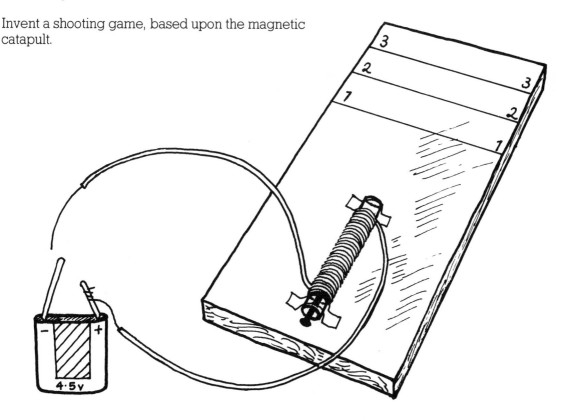

In the classic science fiction novel *Ralph 124C 41+*, by Hugo Gernsback, published in 1911, trains are accelerated to incredible speeds along a sub-Atlantic tunnel, between Britain and America, by passing them through a series of powerful solenoids. Successive solenoids are energized only briefly, as the train enters – otherwise the magnets would slow the train down. Perhaps this clever idea will be used one day.

Splitting water with electricity

You can use electricity to show that water is made from two different gases.

Obtain two carbon rods from inside old battery cells. These will be used as *electrodes*. Bind one end of each electrode *very tightly* with a bared end of a 16 in lead of plastic-covered wire. Then bind around where the connections are made, using electricians' insulating tape. No bared wire should show.

bind end of electrode with bared wire

bind wire with insulating tape

Next, you need two ordinary-size test-tubes (borrowed from a science teacher) and a jar with a wide top. Nearly fill the jar with water – and add half an eggcupful of vinegar (to make the water a better conductor of electricity).

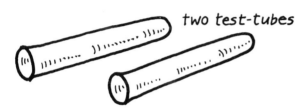

two test-tubes

jar with wide neck

Put the carbon electrodes inside the water-filled jar. Fill a tube to its brim with tap water. Keep your finger over the opening of the tube, while you turn it upside-down and poke its open (but still covered) end under water. No water should fall out and no air get into the tube. Rest this tube over one of the electrodes. Do exactly the same with the other tube, but put it over the second electrode. Connect the leads to a 6 volt battery.

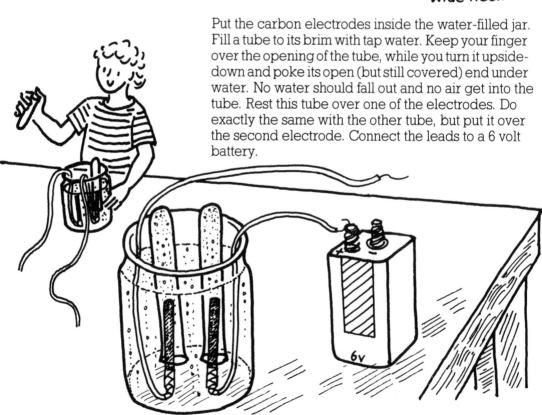

Electric current splits the water into two gases. These fizz up into the tubes over the electrodes. The gases collect in the inverted tubes by pushing down the water levels. After an hour or more you will see that more gas (roughly twice as much) collects over the electrode connected to the negative terminal of the battery.

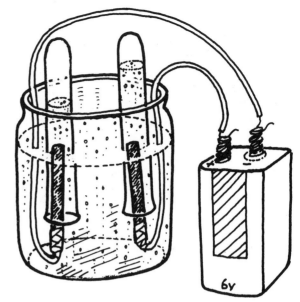

Testing the gases

If you put a finger over the mouth of a tube, before removing it from the water, you can do a test to identify the gas. Turn the tube upright, without removing your finger.

Test the tube with the most gas. Hold it just below a candle flame. Then take away your finger. The gas escapes into the flame and explodes with a loud pop (and, perhaps, a squeaky sound). This gas is *hydrogen*.

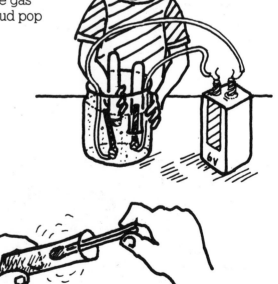

Test the smaller quantity of gas with a glowing match (one you have just lit and blown out). Poke the match into the tube mouth. It should relight. This shows that the other gas is *oxygen*.

You have been doing electrical chemistry, or *electrolysis*. And you have shown evidence that water is made of two gases: hydrogen and oxygen – with twice as much hydrogen.

Joining a resistance

Unwind the nichrome high-resistance wire from a filament of an old space heater element. Wind about 50 in of this wire on to a pencil. The coils of this bare wire must be neatly spaced. Bind the ends of the wire to the ends of the pencil, using insulating tape. Let one end of the wire project for an inch and a half beyond the binding tape.

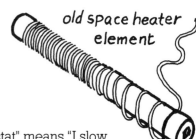

old space heater element

This is a rheostat, a variable electrical resistance. "Rheostat" means "I slow down the stream". It will slow the stream of current (and therefore lessen the amperage), to control the brightness of a lamp, or the speed of an electric motor.

Connect the resistance, in series, with a 3.5 volt bulb in a holder and a 4.5 volt battery. Connect a loose lead to the spare terminal of the battery.

4.5v

Complete the circuit by moving the bared other end of the lead to and fro along the coils of the rheostat. The light should come on and vary in brightness, depending on how far the current has to travel through the resistance wire.

The more resistance, the slower the current, and the less is the amperage (rate of flow of current) to light the bulb.

Use a small electric motor (get one to go with a pressure of 4.5 volts) and see how you can vary its speed with the rheostat.

A hot-wire cutter for making plastic animals

For the last project in this book you need about a yard of thin *constantan* resistance wire. A friendly science teacher will be helpful, no doubt.

You also need to make a U-frame from pieces of wood, glued together. The frame should be about 10 in long, with a gap 5 in wide. Force small nails into the ends of the U-frame. Fix a short piece of the resistance wire between the nails. Connect the nails to 20 in leads made of plastic-insulated wire. Wind the leads a few times round the prongs of the frame, to keep them away from the resistance wire.

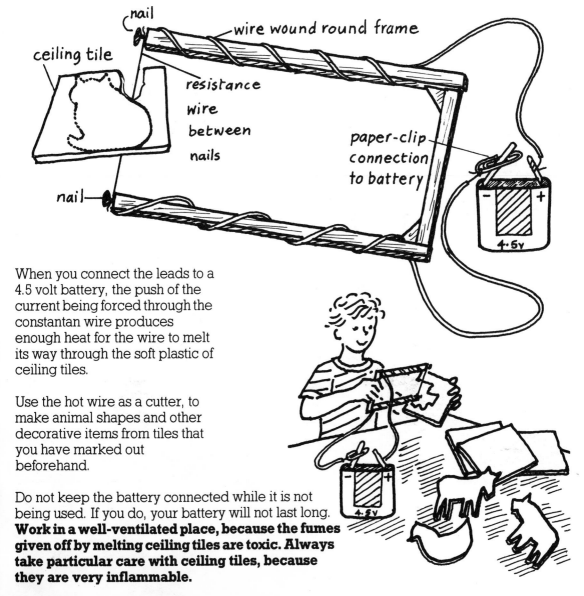

When you connect the leads to a 4.5 volt battery, the push of the current being forced through the constantan wire produces enough heat for the wire to melt its way through the soft plastic of ceiling tiles.

Use the hot wire as a cutter, to make animal shapes and other decorative items from tiles that you have marked out beforehand.

Do not keep the battery connected while it is not being used. If you do, your battery will not last long. **Work in a well-ventilated place, because the fumes given off by melting ceiling tiles are toxic. Always take particular care with ceiling tiles, because they are very inflammable.**

Index